DOLLHOUSE FUN!

Furniture You Can Make

Written by Judith Conaway
Illustrated by Renzo Barto

Troll Associates

Library of Congress Cataloging in Publication Data

Conaway, Judith (date)
    Dollhouse fun!

    Summary: Instructions for making projects to
furnish and decorate a dollhouse.
        1. Doll furniture—Juvenile literature.
2. Dollhouses—Juvenile literature. [1. Doll
furniture.   2. Dollhouses.   3. Handicraft]
I. Barto, Renzo, jll.   II. Title.
TT175.5.C66   1987   745.592′3   86-16133
ISBN 0-8167-0862-2 (lib. bdg.)
ISBN 0-8167-0863-0 (pbk.)

10   9   8   7   6   5   4   3   2   1

CONTENTS

DOLLHOUSE FUN: AN INTRODUCTION

Making your own dollhouse furniture can be both fun and easy! In this book, you'll find many ideas for furnishing and decorating a dollhouse. Some of the projects are based on simple patterns. Others are made from objects that are easily found around your home. *Presto!* A Styrofoam cup becomes a small chair. A soft sponge makes a perfect mattress for a tiny bed. Once you begin, you'll find all sorts of dollhouse decorations can be made from small, everyday items. Start with the ideas in this book. Then go on to create your own! Have fun!

CRAFTS TIPS

Are you just starting out as a furniture designer? Here are some tips on tracing, cutting, gluing, and painting.

Tips on tracing:

Here's a good way to transfer a pattern from this book onto cardboard.

1 Tape a sheet of tracing paper to the page you want to copy. Use a soft pencil, such as a Number 2, and trace the pattern. Do not press too hard.

2 Turn the tracing paper over and rub the pencil over the area where the pattern shows.

3 Turn over the tracing paper and place it on top of a piece of cardboard. Carefully, retrace the shape.

4 Remove the tracing paper. You now have a copy of the pattern.

Safe ways to cut cardboard:

The easiest way to cut corrugated cardboard is to cut across the ridges, or cut between the ridges.

To cut a shape from the center of a piece of cardboard, first trace the shape onto the cardboard, as explained on page 6. The safest way to cut out the shape is to cut in from the outside edge of the cardboard. Then cut around the shape. You can fix the cut edge with tape or glue, if necessary.

Another good way to cut out a shape from cardboard is to use a nail. Press the point of the nail into the center of the shape. Widen the hole with the nail until your scissors will fit inside the hole. Using scissors, cut in a spiral, as shown.

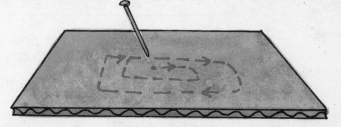

(*Note:* Do *not* use the point of the scissors to start the hole. The handles could slip and cause an accident.)

Gluing without grief:

Gluing can be a big mess! Here's how to handle it.

1 Always spread newspapers over your work area before you begin.

2 Use the right amount of glue. Spread a thin, even layer of glue over the surface to be glued. It's especially important to put glue on the edges.

3 Use a finger tip to spread the glue. Or you can use a paintbrush. Keep a small jar of water handy. Rinse the paintbrush in the water to keep it soft.

4 Weight larger things down with books, while the glue dries. Always let the glue dry *completely* before painting or going on to the next step of a project.

A good paint job makes a pretty big mess! Some tips:

1 Always spread newspapers over the surface where you are going to paint. For big projects, wear a smock or old clothes. Keep rags and paper towels handy for clean-up.

2 Use paints that mix with water. This makes cleaning up easier. Powder paints and poster paints are especially good.

3 Mix your paints in small jars that have screw-on lids. Use ice-cream sticks or plastic spoons—*not* brushes—to mix paint. Mix all the colors you need before you begin a project.

4 Keep plenty of water handy when you paint. Rinse your brushes right after you use them.

BASIC IS BEAUTIFUL:
DOLLHOUSES YOU CAN MAKE

Some of the very best dollhouses are not the ones you buy, but the ones you make yourself. Here are a few basic ideas to get you started.

A large, sturdy cardboard or wooden box makes an excellent one-room dollhouse. Glue wrapping paper in place for wallpaper, or cover the walls with poster paint. You're ready to fill the room with your small creations.

Add on to your one room with more boxes. You can stack them or place them side by side. Soon you'll have a complete house.

To make your rooms look just right, try these ideas:

Doors should be long and rectangular. The top of the door should be quite close to the ceiling.

A double line, as shown, is the door frame. Windows should line up with the top of the door frame. A line around the base of the walls is the baseboard.

Fit a piece of construction paper on the floor. A bright color can be used as a rug. Or a tan sheet with black lines drawn on it can look like a wooden floor. Add a scrap of rug for a throw rug, if you like.

You can also add picture frames or candles to the walls. They can be drawn right on the walls or cut from another piece of construction paper and glued in place.

Boxes can be used for a roof and chimney. Cut
and glue in place, as shown.

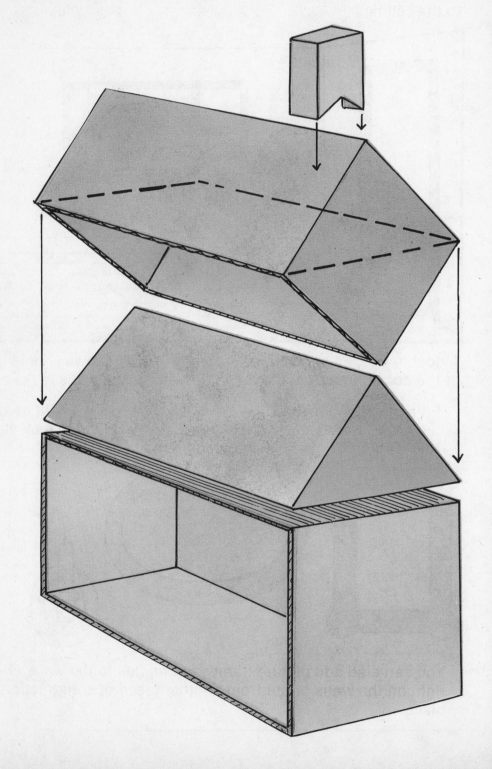

To add a dormer, cut a small box, as shown. Use markers or paints to add a window to your dormer, and glue it to the roof.

Color your chimney red and add a brick pattern to it.

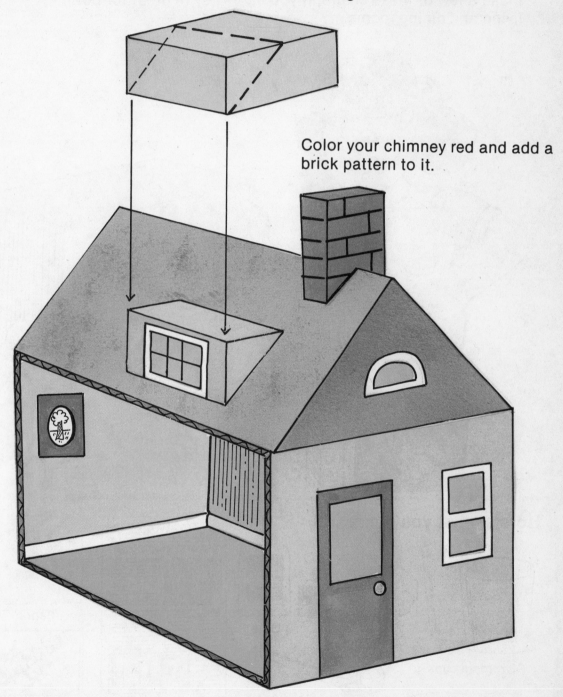

Use markers to add any details you wish to the outside of your dollhouse.

BUCKET CHAIR

Make a few of these chairs, if you like. They're great for both living and dining rooms.

Here's what you need:

Styrofoam cups

Cotton balls

Glue

Pencil

Scissors

Newspapers

Fabric

Tracing paper

Here's what you do:

1 Copy this pattern onto a piece of paper, and cut it out. Line up the top of the pattern with the top of a Styrofoam cup, as shown. Cut the pattern out of the cup. Trim off any slivers of Styrofoam.

2 Turn another Styrofoam cup upside down and trace a circle on a piece of fabric. Cut out the circle.

3 Place the fabric circle on top of some newspapers. Put a line of glue around the edge of the circle. Then put several cotton balls in the center of the fabric.

4 Fold the glued edge of the circle over the stuffing to make a small pillow. Squeeze the fabric tightly together, while the glue dries. Turn the pillow over, and stuff it firmly into your bucket chair.

SPONGE SOFA

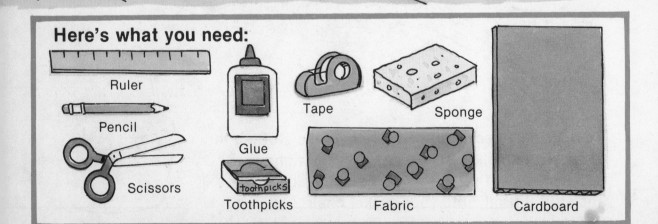

Here's what you need:

Ruler

Pencil

Scissors

Glue

Toothpicks

Tape

Sponge

Fabric

Cardboard

Here's what you do:

1 Measure and mark a line along the long side of a sponge about 1″ in from the edge. Wet the sponge and squeeze it dry. Then cut the sponge along the line. Let the sponge dry. The bigger piece will be the seat of your sofa. The smaller piece is the backrest.

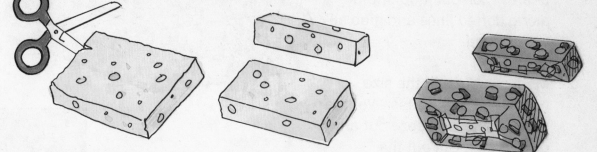

2 Cover the two pieces of sponge with fabric. Tape the fabric underneath the sponges.

3 Cut a long strip of cardboard about 1″ wide. Fold it to form a rectangle with a small tab. The rectangle should be slightly smaller than the sofa seat. Glue the tab closed.

4 Place a toothpick into each corner of the cardboard. Push the two front toothpicks into the bottom of the sofa seat. Push the two rear toothpicks up through the seat to attach the backrest.

17

BED

Here's what you do:

1 Copy the bed pattern onto cardboard. Then cut it out. Fold along dotted lines and glue all tabs closed.

2 Mark a sponge to the size needed for a mattress. Wet the sponge, then squeeze out any extra water. Cut out the mattress and let dry.

Here's what you need:

Fabric or cloth handkerchief

Scissors

Pencil

Glue

Sponge

Cardboard

Tab

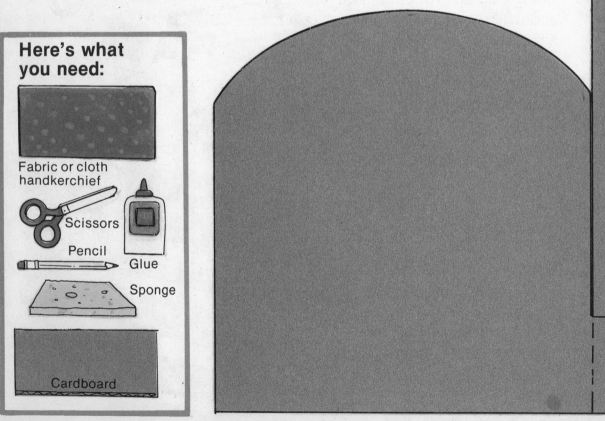

3 Apply glue beneath the sponge and place it on the bed. Allow glue to dry.

4 If you like, add a handkerchief or a piece of fabric for a bedspread.

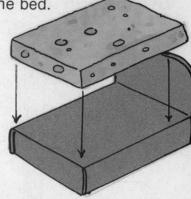

Tab

Bed pattern

Tab

BOOKCASE

Here's what you need:

Pencil

Scissors

Glue

Cardboard

Here's what you do:

1 Copy the bookcase and shelf patterns onto cardboard. Cut out the shapes and fold along all dotted lines.

2 Glue all tabs on bookcase and let dry. Then glue the shelf in place, as shown.

Shelf

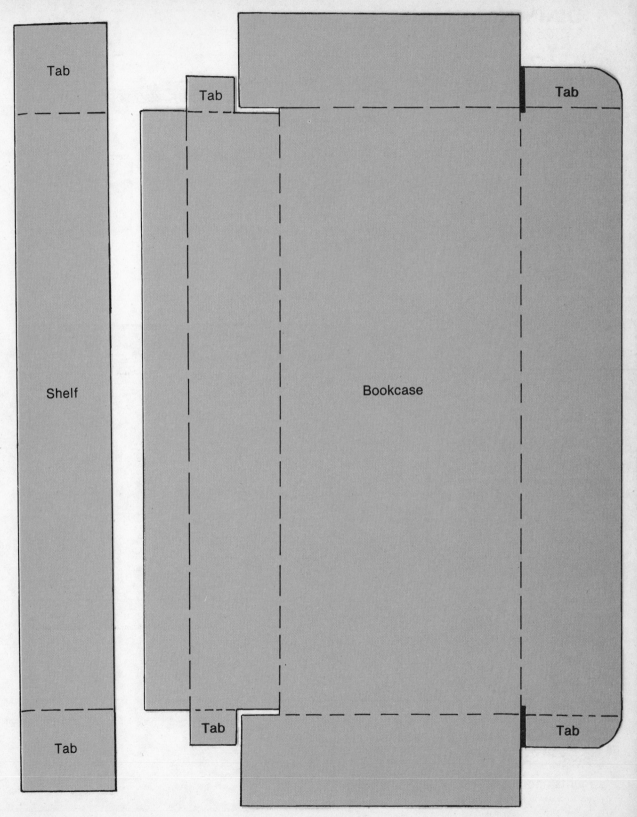

DINING-ROOM HUTCH

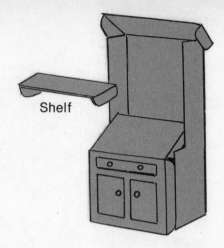

Shelf

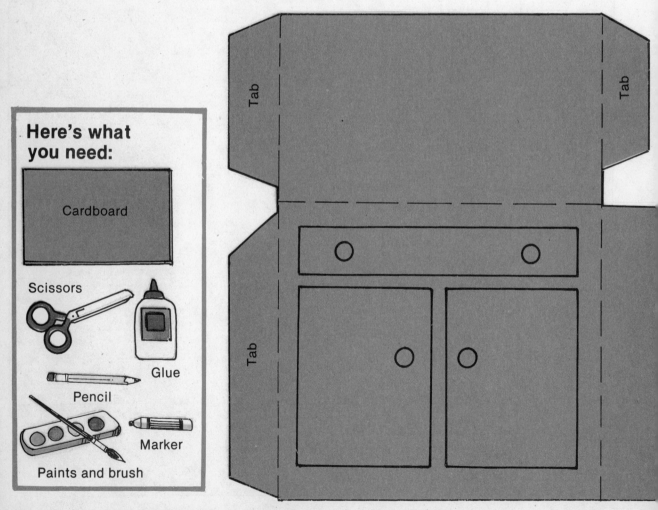

Tab

Tab

Tab

Tab

Tab

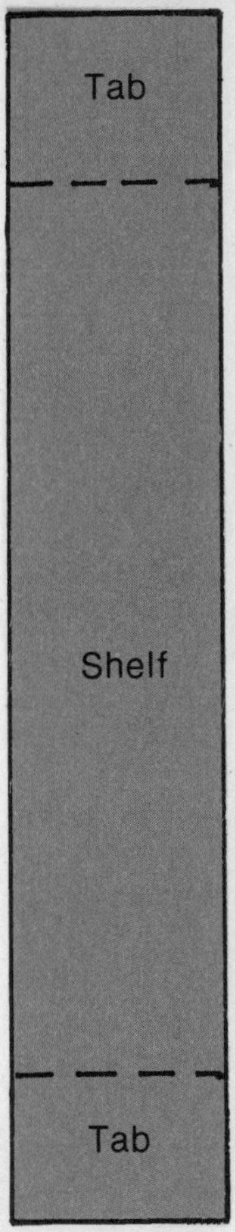

Tab

Shelf

Tab

Here's what you do:

1   Copy the pattern for the hutch
and shelf onto cardboard. Cut out
the shapes and fold along all
dotted lines.

2   Glue the tabs on the hutch into
place and let dry.

3   Next, put glue on the shelf tabs
and attach them to the hutch.

4   Use a marker and paints to add a
few details to your hutch.

ROCKING CHAIR

Here's what you need:

Pencil

Markers

Scissors

Glue

Cardboard

Here's what you do:

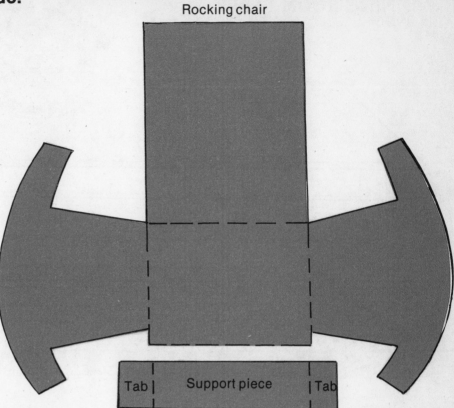

Rocking chair

Tab | Support piece | Tab

1 Copy this pattern for the rocking chair onto cardboard. Cut out both the chair and the support piece.

2 Fold along the dotted lines. Then glue the support piece beneath the chair, as shown.

3 Color or add pretty designs to your rocking chair with markers.

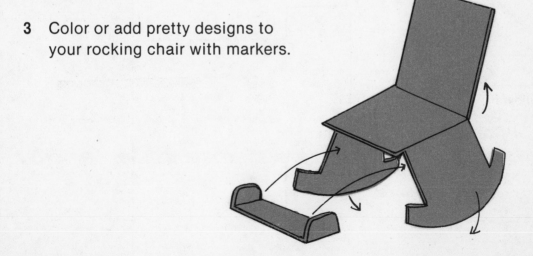

DINING-ROOM TABLE

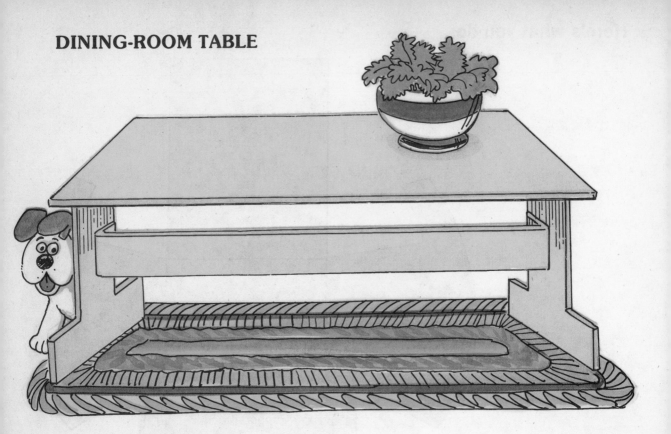

Here's what you need:

Cardboard

Scissors

Glue

Pencil

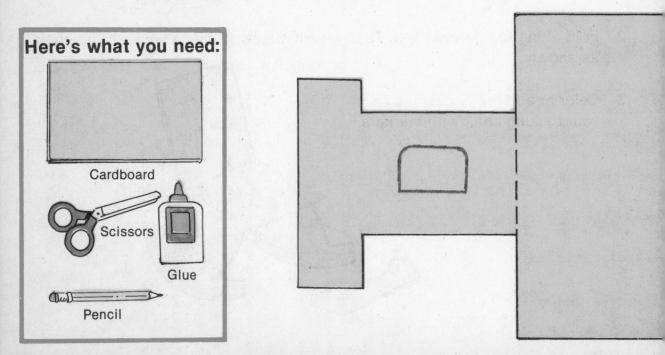

Here's what you do:

1 Copy the patterns for the table and support piece onto cardboard. Cut them out.

2 Fold along all dotted lines. Then glue the support piece's two tabs to the legs of the table. (Red lines on table legs show where tabs should be placed.)

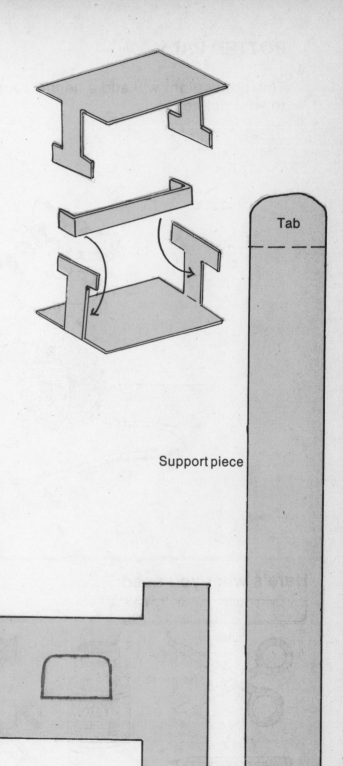

Support piece

Table

Tab

Tab

POTTED PALM

This pretty plant will add a homey touch to your dollhouse.

Here's what you need:

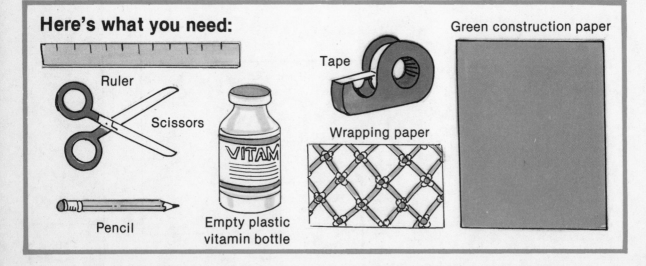

Ruler

Scissors

Pencil

Empty plastic vitamin bottle

Tape

Wrapping paper

Green construction paper

Here's what you do:

1   Cut a strip of green construction paper to measure about 8″ wide × 6″ tall.

2   Cut the outline of the leaves in long V-shapes, as shown. (*Note:* Do not cut all the way to the bottom of the paper—leave about 2″ of space.)

3   Coil the row of leaves tightly around a pencil. Hold the rolled leaves together, and remove the pencil. Then put the palm into an empty plastic vitamin bottle.

4   Cut a strip of wrapping paper. Wrap it around the bottle, and tape in place.

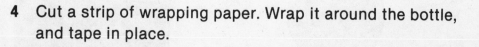

ROUND TABLE

Here's what you need:

Pencil

Tape

Glue

Scissors

Plastic coffee-can lid

Cardboard

Here's what you do:

1 Copy the pattern for the legs onto cardboard. Cut it out, and fold along the dotted lines. Glue the tab in place, as shown. Then wait for the glue to dry.

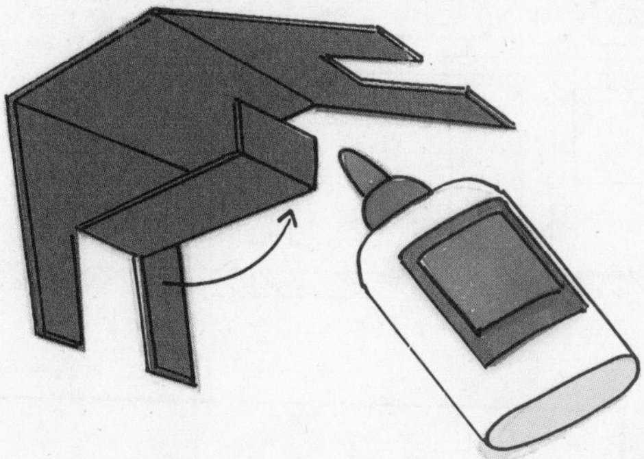

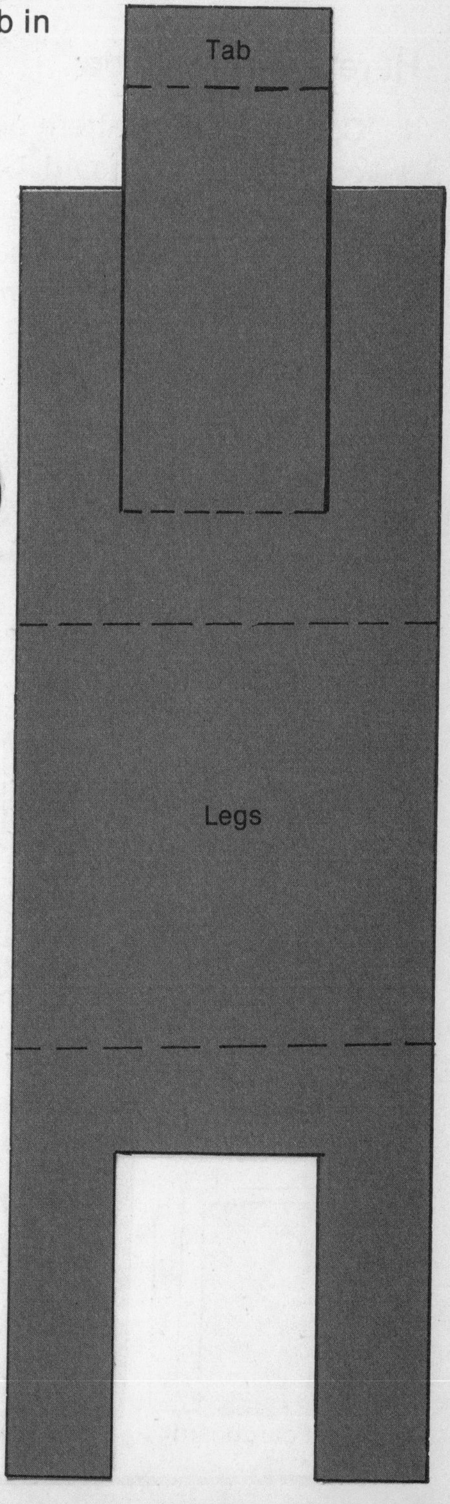

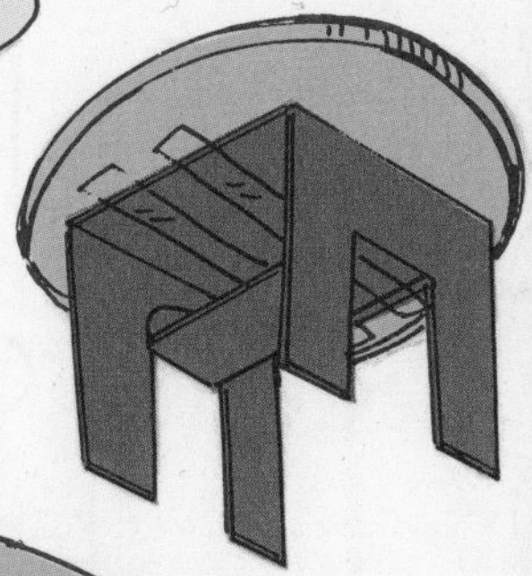

2 Tape the legs to the underside of the plastic lid. Your table is ready!

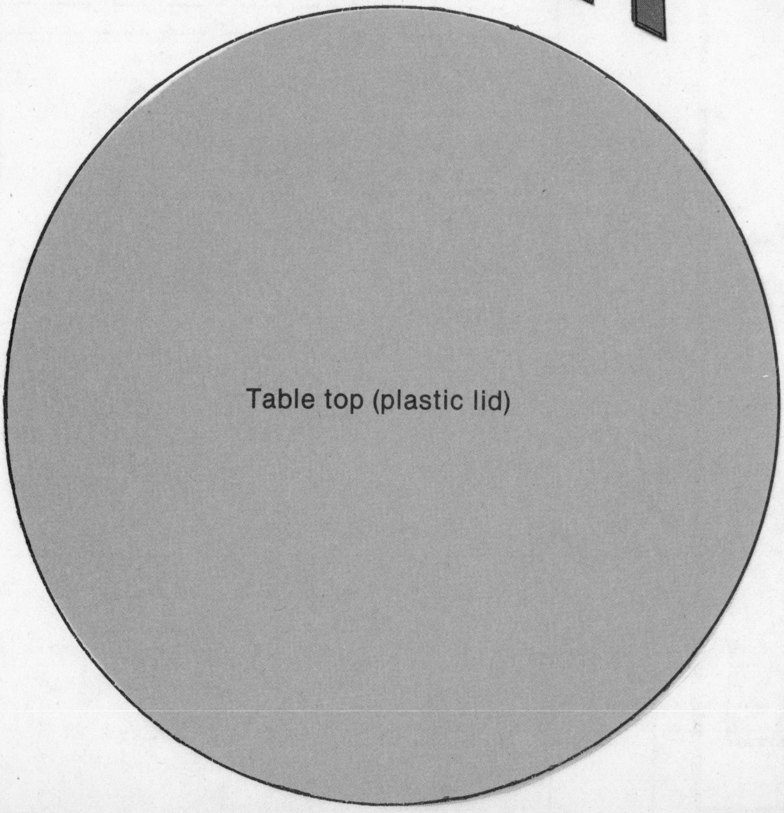

Tab

Legs

Table top (plastic lid)

DOLLHOUSE OVEN

Here's what you do:

1 Copy the oven pattern onto corrugated cardboard. Cut it out. Fold along all dotted lines. Using a marker, draw the oven door, burners, and controls.

Here's what you need for the projects on pages 32-37:

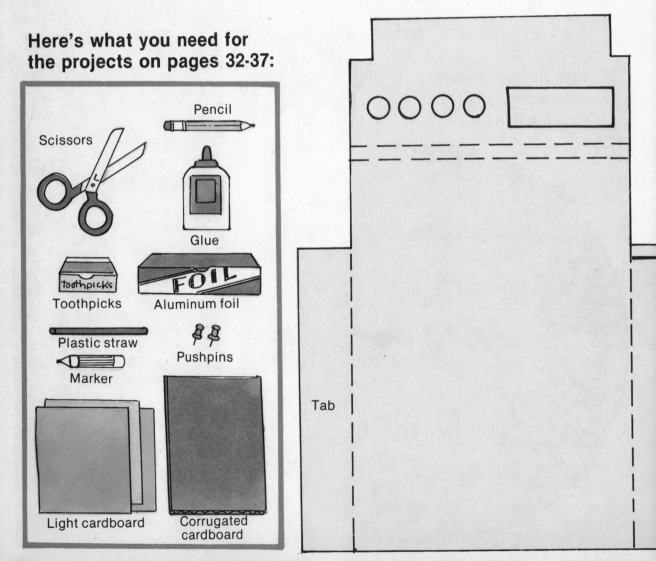

Pencil

Scissors

Glue

Toothpicks

Aluminum foil

Plastic straw

Pushpins

Marker

Light cardboard

Corrugated cardboard

Tab

2 Glue the tabs shut.

3 To make the oven-door handle, cut a 2″ length of plastic straw. Using a pushpin, make holes at each end of the straw. Then find the handle pictured on the oven door and make two holes in the cardboard, where shown. Take two short bits of toothpick and place each one through the holes in the straw and then into the holes in the oven door.

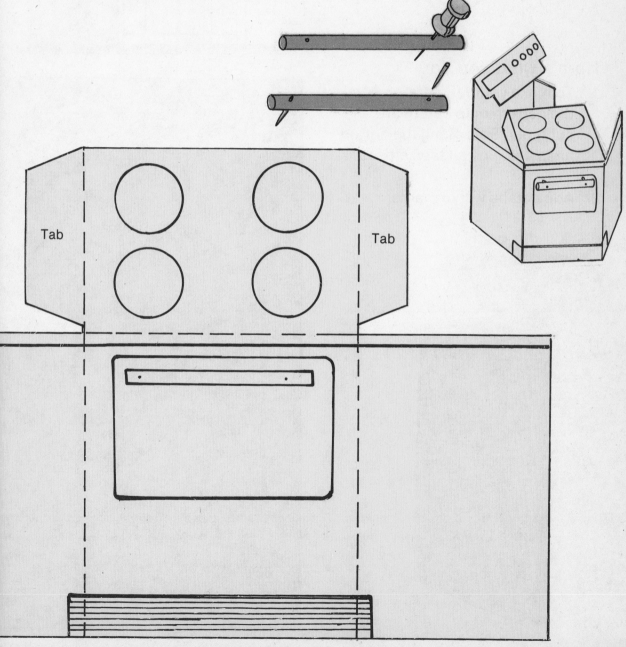

DOLLHOUSE REFRIGERATOR

Here's what you do:

1   To make your refrigerator, copy the pattern onto cardboard and cut it out. Fold along the dotted lines and glue all tabs closed.

2   Add details with a marker.

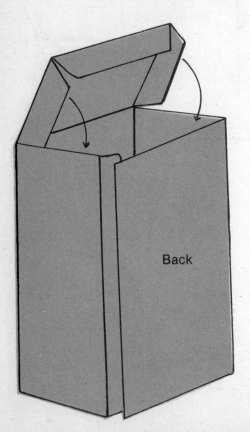

Back

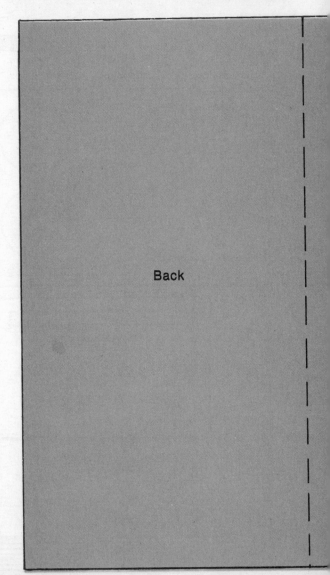

Back

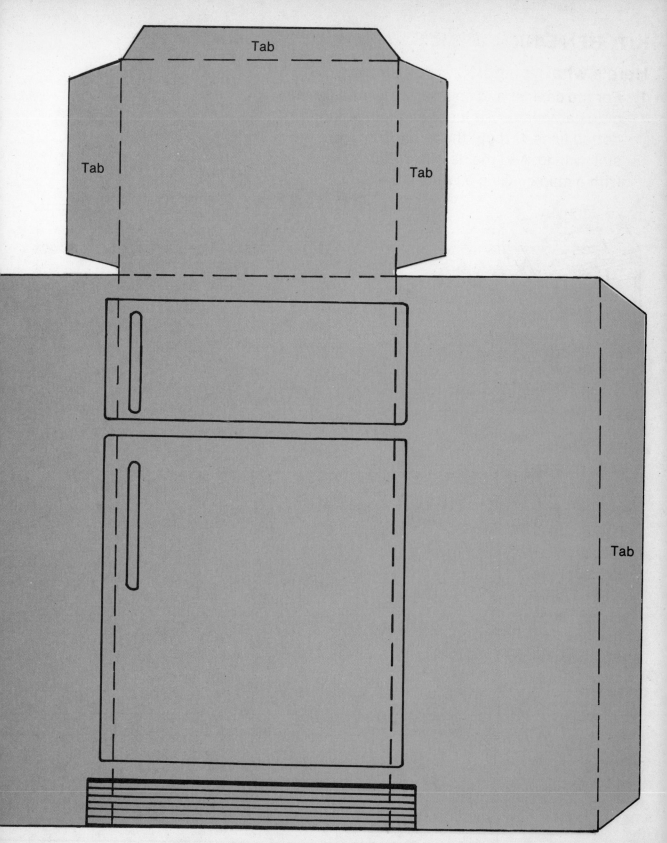

KITCHEN SINK

Here's what you do:

1 For the cabinet and counter, copy this pattern onto cardboard. Cut it out and fold along dotted lines. Cut out the rectangle where the sink will go. Add the details of the drawers with a marker. Glue all tabs closed.

Cabinet and counter

2 To make the sink, copy the pattern on lightweight cardboard. Cut it out. Draw a circle for the drain. Fold as shown, and put the sink into the counter top. Glue all tabs in place.

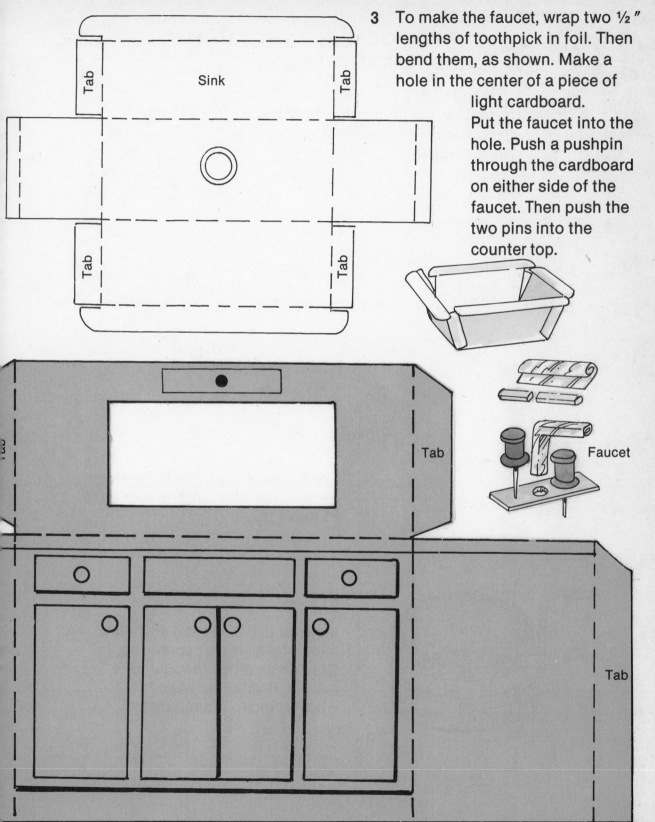

3 To make the faucet, wrap two ½″ lengths of toothpick in foil. Then bend them, as shown. Make a hole in the center of a piece of light cardboard.

Put the faucet into the hole. Push a pushpin through the cardboard on either side of the faucet. Then push the two pins into the counter top.

Sink

Tab

Tab

Tab

Tab

Faucet

Tab

Tab

QUICK IDEAS FOR THE KITCHEN AND DINING ROOM

Use the tops of toothpaste tubes for tiny drinking glasses.

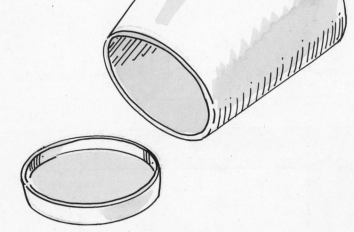

For plates, cut off the bottoms of paper cups. Cut larger paper cups to make trays.

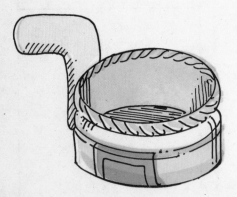

Make pots from metal soft-drink caps (the kind that screw on). Glue on an elbow noodle for a handle. If you like, wrap the whole thing in aluminum foil.

Bowls can be made from an egg carton. Cut out the bottoms of the egg holders for mixing bowls. Smaller bowls can be cut from the sections between the egg holders.

Glue noodles together to make a fancy candlestick holder for your dining-room table. Cut "candles" from a cardboard lollipop stick or cotton swab. Place the candles in the noodles. Fill the space between each noodle and its candle with glue.

For a garbage can, use a plastic film container with a snap-on lid.

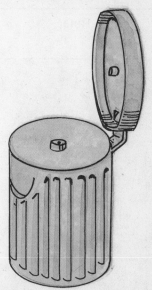

DESK

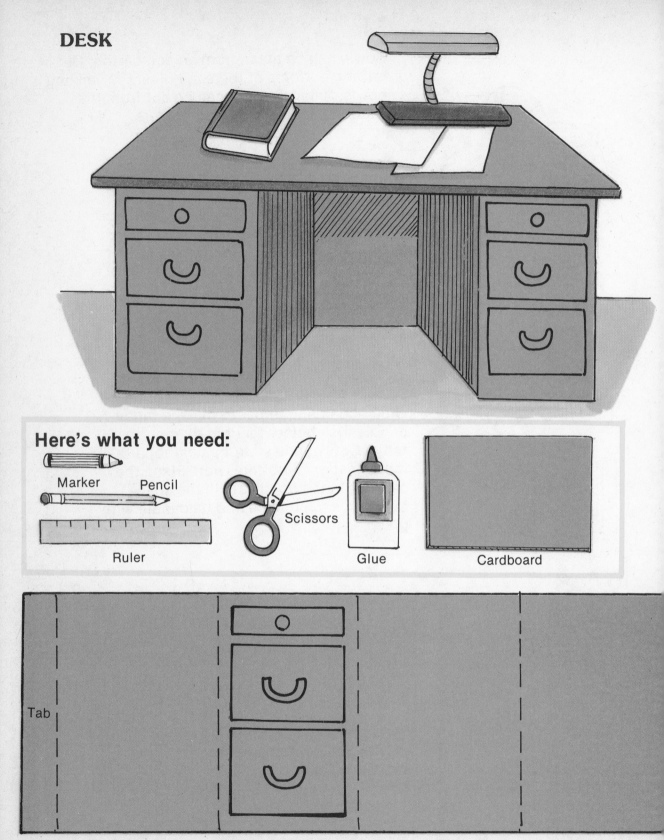

Here's what you need:

Marker   Pencil

Ruler

Scissors

Glue

Cardboard

Tab

Here's what you do:

1 Copy the patterns for the drawers and desk top onto cardboard. Cut them out. Fold the drawers along the dotted lines and glue the tabs shut. Let the glue dry. Use a marker to draw the drawers and other details.

2 Apply a bead of glue to the desk top, as shown. Then place the desk top on the drawers. Allow the glue to dry.

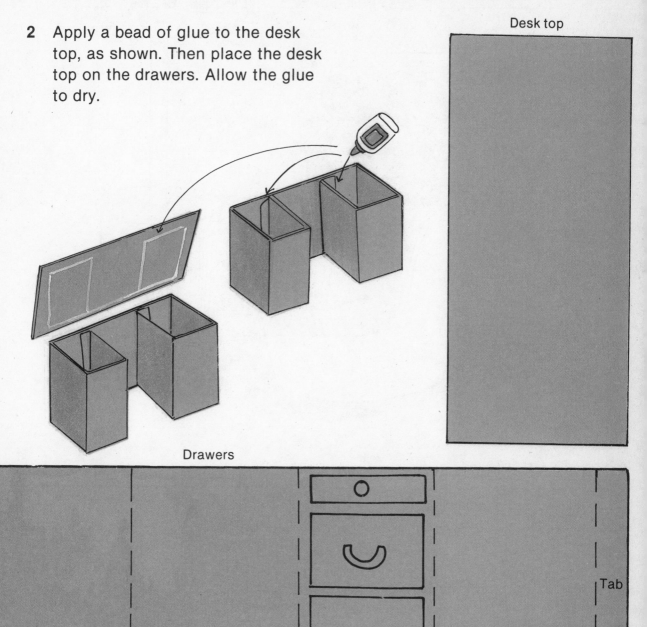

Desk top

Drawers

Tab

PRETTY LAMP

Here's what you need:

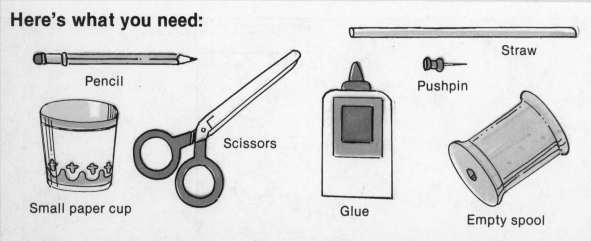

Pencil

Straw

Pushpin

Scissors

Small paper cup

Glue

Empty spool

Here's what you do:

1 Cut off the top two-thirds of a small paper cup.

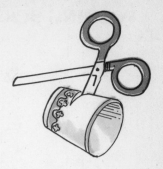

2 Cut a length of drinking straw—a short length for a desk lamp or a longer piece for a floor lamp.

3 Use a pushpin to start a hole in the center of the cup. Using the point of a pencil, enlarge the hole until a straw will fit snugly into it.

4 Insert the other end of the straw into the opening of a spool.

5 Apply a bead of glue around the top of the lamp shade to hold it to the straw.

FOLDING SCREEN

Here's what you need:

Scissors

Adhesive tape

Pencil

Ruler

Cardboard

Glue

Wrapping paper or scrap of wallpaper

Here's what you do:

1 Cut out five strips of cardboard like this one, each measuring 1″×6″.

2 Cut out five strips of wrapping paper or wallpaper, each measuring 1″×6″. Glue each strip of paper to a strip of cardboard.

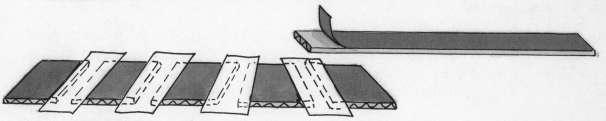

3 Join the front of the panels together with adhesive tape. Fold the extra tape around the back of the panels.

4 Turn the screen over. Reinforce each joint with a length of tape. Press the front and back tapes together between the panels, as shown.

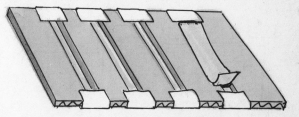

5 Carefully, bend the panels in a zigzag. The finished screen folds back and forth like this.

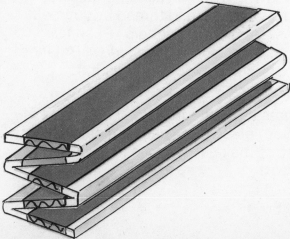

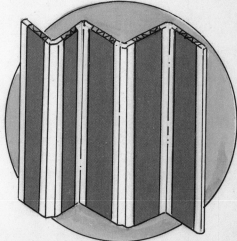

EXCELLENT EXTRAS

These little extra touches will make your dollhouse special.

Collect some pretty postage stamps. They make nice pictures for the walls of your dollhouse. Or you can paint your own small pictures. Frame them by gluing each picture to a small rectangle of construction paper, as shown. Then glue or tape them to your dollhouse walls. Small pictures cut from magazines also look nice.

A wall clock is a homey touch. You can use an old toy wristwatch—it's the perfect size.

Hang some curtains on those small windows. Cloth hankies or squares of fabric can be cut to the size you need. Use a straw or pipe cleaner as a curtain rod. Fold the edge of the curtain over the rod. With a needle and thread, sew the curtain around the rod by making a small hem, as shown. (*Note:* If you're not allowed to use a needle and thread by yourself, ask a grownup for help.) Push two pushpins above the window. Balance your curtain rod over the pins.

Make your rooms cozy by adding rugs and mats to the floors. Old or extra bits of carpet or linoleum work well. Old woven or cloth place mats can also easily be cut down to the size you need. Small straw coasters make good mats for your floors. Or try a doily or old washcloth—they look great!